this journal belongs to:

Today I'm grateful for:

1 My family

2 pretty flowers

3 my pet

How to use this journal:

How am I today?

Todays weather:

Something Good

Pizza for Dinner

Something New

we have a new kid in our class

This is how I was kind today:

I told my teacher her dress was pretty

This is how I was helpful today:

Did extra chores after dinner

Draw Here

Get creative - draw whatever you want

Inhale and say "I am" - exhale and say the words below - then check it off

I AM....

☑ BRAVE   ☑ KIND

CONFIDENT
☑

☑ HELPFUL   ☑ STRONG   ☑ SMART

☑ ENOUGH   ☑ LOVED   ☑ HONEST

Extra Thoughts

I have a spelling test on Friday. I'm nervous but

will try my best.

Today I'm grateful for:

1

2

3

How am I today?

Todays weather:

Something Good

Something New

This is how I was kind today:

This is how I was helpful today:

Draw Here

I AM....

☐ BRAVE

☐ KIND

CONFIDENT
☐

☐ HELPFUL

☐ STRONG

☐ SMART

☐ ENOUGH

☐ LOVED

☐ HONEST

Extra Thoughts

Today I'm grateful for:

1

2

3

Date:

How am I today?

Todays weather:

Something Good

Something New

This is how I was kind today:

This is how I was helpful today:

Draw Here

I AM....

☐ BRAVE   ☐ KIND

CONFIDENT
☐

☐ HELPFUL   ☐ STRONG   ☐ SMART

☐ ENOUGH   ☐ LOVED   ☐ HONEST

Extra Thoughts

Today I'm grateful for:

1

2

3

How am I today?

Todays weather:

Something Good

Something New

This is how I was kind today:

This is how I was helpful today:

Draw Here

I AM....

☐ BRAVE   ☐ KIND

CONFIDENT
☐

☐ HELPFUL   ☐ STRONG   ☐ SMART

☐ ENOUGH   ☐ LOVED   ☐ HONEST

Extra Thoughts

Today I'm grateful for:

1

2

3

Date:

How am I today?

Todays weather:

Something Good

Something New

This is how I was kind today:

This is how I was helpful today:

Draw Here

I AM....

- ☐ BRAVE
- ☐ KIND
- ☐ CONFIDENT
- ☐ HELPFUL
- ☐ STRONG
- ☐ SMART
- ☐ ENOUGH
- ☐ LOVED
- ☐ HONEST

Extra Thoughts

Today I'm grateful for:

1

2

3

Date:

How am I today?

Todays weather:

Something Good

Something New

This is how I was kind today:

This is how I was helpful today:

Draw Here

I AM....

- ☐ BRAVE
- ☐ KIND
- CONFIDENT ☐
- ☐ HELPFUL
- ☐ STRONG
- ☐ SMART
- ☐ ENOUGH
- ☐ LOVED
- ☐ HONEST

↘ Extra Thoughts ↙

Today I'm grateful for:

1.

2.

3.

Date: _____

How am I today?

Todays weather:

Something Good

Something New

This is how I was kind today:

This is how I was helpful today:

Draw Here

I AM....

☐ BRAVE   ☐ KIND

CONFIDENT
☐

☐ HELPFUL   ☐ STRONG   ☐ SMART

☐ ENOUGH   ☐ LOVED   ☐ HONEST

Extra Thoughts

Today I'm grateful for:

1

2

3

Date:

How am I today?

Todays weather:

Something Good

Something New

This is how I was kind today:

This is how I was helpful today:

I AM....

- ☐ BRAVE
- ☐ KIND
- CONFIDENT ☐
- ☐ HELPFUL
- ☐ STRONG
- ☐ SMART
- ☐ ENOUGH
- ☐ LOVED
- ☐ HONEST

Extra Thoughts

Today I'm grateful for:

1

2

3

Date:

How am I today?

Todays weather:

Something Good

Something New

This is how I was Kind today:

This is how I was helpful today:

Draw Here

I AM....

☐ BRAVE   ☐ KIND

CONFIDENT
☐

☐ HELPFUL   ☐ STRONG   ☐ SMART

☐ ENOUGH   ☐ LOVED   ☐ HONEST

Extra Thoughts

Today I'm grateful for:

1

2

3

How am I today?

Todays weather:

Something Good

Something New

This is how I was Kind today:

This is how I was helpful today:

I AM....

□ BRAVE □ KIND

CONFIDENT
□

□ HELPFUL □ STRONG □ SMART

□ ENOUGH □ LOVED □ HONEST

Extra Thoughts

Today I'm grateful for:

1

2

3

How am I today?

Todays weather:

Something Good

Something New

This is how I was kind today:

This is how I was helpful today:

Draw Here

I AM....

☐ BRAVE   ☐ KIND

CONFIDENT
☐

☐ HELPFUL   ☐ STRONG   ☐ SMART

☐ ENOUGH   ☐ LOVED   ☐ HONEST

↘ Extra Thoughts ↙

Today I'm grateful for:

1

2

3

Date:

How am I today?

Todays weather:

Something Good

Something New

This is how I was kind today:

This is how I was helpful today:

I AM....

☐ BRAVE   ☐ KIND

CONFIDENT
☐

☐ HELPFUL   ☐ STRONG   ☐ SMART

☐ ENOUGH   ☐ LOVED   ☐ HONEST

Extra Thoughts

Today I'm grateful for:

1

2

3

Date:

How am I today?

Todays weather:

Something Good

Something New

This is how I was kind today:

This is how I was helpful today:

Draw Here

I AM....

□ BRAVE   □ KIND

CONFIDENT
□

□ HELPFUL   □ STRONG   □ SMART

□ ENOUGH   □ LOVED   □ HONEST

Extra Thoughts

Today I'm grateful for:

1

2

3

Date:

How am I today?

Todays weather:

Something Good

Something New

This is how I was kind today:

This is how I was helpful today:

I AM....

- ☐ BRAVE
- ☐ KIND
- ☐ CONFIDENT
- ☐ HELPFUL
- ☐ STRONG
- ☐ SMART
- ☐ ENOUGH
- ☐ LOVED
- ☐ HONEST

Extra Thoughts

Today I'm grateful for:

1

2

3

Date:

How am I today?

Todays weather:

Something Good

Something New

This is how I was kind today:

This is how I was helpful today:

Draw Here

I AM....

☐ BRAVE   ☐ KIND

CONFIDENT
☐

☐ HELPFUL   ☐ STRONG   ☐ SMART

☐ ENOUGH   ☐ LOVED   ☐ HONEST

Extra Thoughts

Today I'm grateful for:

1

2

3

How am I today?

Todays weather:

Something Good

Something New

This is how I was kind today:

This is how I was helpful today:

 Draw Here

I AM....

- ☐ BRAVE
- ☐ KIND
- ☐ CONFIDENT
- ☐ HELPFUL
- ☐ STRONG
- ☐ SMART
- ☐ ENOUGH
- ☐ LOVED
- ☐ HONEST

Extra Thoughts

Today I'm grateful for:

1

2

3

How am I today?

Todays weather:

Something Good

Something New

This is how I was Kind today:

This is how I was helpful today:

Draw Here

I AM....

☐ BRAVE   ☐ KIND

CONFIDENT
☐

☐ HELPFUL   ☐ STRONG   ☐ SMART

☐ ENOUGH   ☐ LOVED   ☐ HONEST

Extra Thoughts

Today I'm grateful for:

1

2

3

Date:

How am I today?

Todays weather:

Something Good

Something New

This is how I was kind today:

This is how I was helpful today:

Draw Here

I AM....

☐ BRAVE   ☐ KIND

CONFIDENT ☐

☐ HELPFUL   ☐ STRONG   ☐ SMART

☐ ENOUGH   ☐ LOVED   ☐ HONEST

Extra Thoughts

Today I'm grateful for:

1

2

3

How am I today?

Todays weather:

Something Good

Something New

This is how I was kind today:

This is how I was helpful today:

Draw Here

I AM....

☐ BRAVE   ☐ KIND

CONFIDENT
☐

☐ HELPFUL   ☐ STRONG   ☐ SMART

☐ ENOUGH   ☐ LOVED   ☐ HONEST

Extra Thoughts

Today I'm grateful for:

1

2

3

Date:

How am I today?

Todays weather:

Something Good

Something New

This is how I was kind today:

This is how I was helpful today:

Draw Here

I AM....

- ☐ BRAVE
- ☐ KIND
- CONFIDENT ☐
- ☐ HELPFUL
- ☐ STRONG
- ☐ SMART
- ☐ ENOUGH
- ☐ LOVED
- ☐ HONEST

Extra Thoughts

Today I'm grateful for:

1

2

3

How am I today?

Todays weather:

Something Good

Something New

This is how I was kind today:

This is how I was helpful today:

Draw Here

I AM....

☐ BRAVE   ☐ KIND

CONFIDENT
☐

☐ HELPFUL   ☐ STRONG   ☐ SMART

☐ ENOUGH   ☐ LOVED   ☐ HONEST

Extra Thoughts

Today I'm grateful for:

1

2

3

Date:

How am I today?

Todays weather:

Something Good

Something New

This is how I was kind today:

This is how I was helpful today:

Draw Here

I AM....

☐ BRAVE

☐ KIND

CONFIDENT
☐

☐ HELPFUL

☐ STRONG

☐ SMART

☐ ENOUGH

☐ LOVED

☐ HONEST

Extra Thoughts

Today I'm grateful for:

1

2

3

Date:

How am I today?

Todays weather:

Something Good

Something New

This is how I was kind today:

This is how I was helpful today:

Draw Here

I AM....

- [ ] BRAVE
- [ ] KIND
- [ ] CONFIDENT
- [ ] HELPFUL
- [ ] STRONG
- [ ] SMART
- [ ] ENOUGH
- [ ] LOVED
- [ ] HONEST

Extra Thoughts

Today I'm grateful for:

1

2

3

Date:

How am I today?

Todays weather:

Something Good

Something New

This is how I was kind today:

This is how I was helpful today:

 Draw Here

I AM....

☐ BRAVE   ☐ KIND

CONFIDENT
☐

☐ HELPFUL   ☐ STRONG   ☐ SMART

☐ ENOUGH   ☐ LOVED   ☐ HONEST

Extra Thoughts

Today I'm grateful for:

1

2

3

Date:

How am I today?

Todays weather:

Something Good

Something New

This is how I was kind today:

This is how I was helpful today:

 Draw Here

I AM....

- ☐ BRAVE
- ☐ KIND
- CONFIDENT ☐
- ☐ HELPFUL
- ☐ STRONG
- ☐ SMART
- ☐ ENOUGH
- ☐ LOVED
- ☐ HONEST

Extra Thoughts

Today I'm grateful for:

1

2

3

How am I today?

Todays weather:

Something Good

Something New

This is how I was kind today:

This is how I was helpful today:

Draw Here

I AM....

- ☐ BRAVE
- ☐ KIND
- ☐ CONFIDENT
- ☐ HELPFUL
- ☐ STRONG
- ☐ SMART
- ☐ ENOUGH
- ☐ LOVED
- ☐ HONEST

Extra Thoughts

Today I'm grateful for:

1

2

3

Date:

How am I today?

Todays weather:

Something Good

Something New

This is how I was kind today:

This is how I was helpful today:

 Draw Here

I AM....

- [ ] BRAVE
- [ ] KIND
- [ ] CONFIDENT
- [ ] HELPFUL
- [ ] STRONG
- [ ] SMART
- [ ] ENOUGH
- [ ] LOVED
- [ ] HONEST

Extra Thoughts

Today I'm grateful for:

1

2

3

Date:

How am I today?

Todays weather:

Something Good

Something New

This is how I was kind today:

This is how I was helpful today:

Draw Here

I AM....

☐ BRAVE ☐ KIND

CONFIDENT ☐

☐ HELPFUL ☐ STRONG ☐ SMART

☐ ENOUGH ☐ LOVED ☐ HONEST

Extra Thoughts

Today I'm grateful for:

1

2

3

How am I today?

Todays weather:

Something Good

Something New

This is how I was kind today:

This is how I was helpful today:

Draw Here

I AM....

- [ ] BRAVE
- [ ] KIND
- [ ] CONFIDENT
- [ ] HELPFUL
- [ ] STRONG
- [ ] SMART
- [ ] ENOUGH
- [ ] LOVED
- [ ] HONEST

Extra Thoughts

Today I'm grateful for:

1

2

3

Date:

How am I today?

Todays weather:

Something Good

Something New

This is how I was kind today:

This is how I was helpful today:

Draw Here

I AM....

☐ BRAVE   ☐ KIND

CONFIDENT
☐

☐ HELPFUL   ☐ STRONG   ☐ SMART

☐ ENOUGH   ☐ LOVED   ☐ HONEST

Extra Thoughts

Today I'm grateful for:

1

2

3

Date:

How am I today?

Todays weather:

Something Good

Something New

This is how I was kind today:

This is how I was helpful today:

Draw Here

I AM....

☐ BRAVE   ☐ KIND

CONFIDENT
☐

☐ HELPFUL   ☐ STRONG   ☐ SMART

☐ ENOUGH   ☐ LOVED   ☐ HONEST

Extra Thoughts

Today I'm grateful for:

1
2
3

How am I today?

Todays weather:

Something Good

Something New

This is how I was kind today:

This is how I was helpful today:

Draw Here

I AM....

☐ BRAVE   ☐ KIND

CONFIDENT
☐

☐ HELPFUL   ☐ STRONG   ☐ SMART

☐ ENOUGH   ☐ LOVED   ☐ HONEST

Extra Thoughts

Today I'm grateful for:

1

2

3

Date:

How am I today?

Todays weather:

Something Good

Something New

This is how I was kind today:

This is how I was helpful today:

Draw Here

I AM....

☐ BRAVE   ☐ KIND

CONFIDENT
☐

☐ HELPFUL   ☐ STRONG   ☐ SMART

☐ ENOUGH   ☐ LOVED   ☐ HONEST

Extra Thoughts

Today I'm grateful for:

1

2

3

How am I today?

Todays weather:

Something Good

Something New

This is how I was kind today:

This is how I was helpful today:

Draw Here

I AM....

- ☐ BRAVE
- ☐ KIND
- ☐ CONFIDENT
- ☐ HELPFUL
- ☐ STRONG
- ☐ SMART
- ☐ ENOUGH
- ☐ LOVED
- ☐ HONEST

Extra Thoughts

Today I'm grateful for:

1

2

3

How am I today?

Todays weather:

Something Good

Something New

This is how I was kind today:

This is how I was helpful today:

Draw Here

I AM....

☐ BRAVE   ☐ KIND

CONFIDENT
☐

☐ HELPFUL   ☐ STRONG   ☐ SMART

☐ ENOUGH   ☐ LOVED   ☐ HONEST

Extra Thoughts

Today I'm grateful for:

1

2

3

How am I today?

Todays weather:

Something Good

Something New

This is how I was kind today:

This is how I was helpful today:

Draw Here

I AM....

☐ BRAVE   ☐ KIND

CONFIDENT
☐

☐ HELPFUL   ☐ STRONG   ☐ SMART

☐ ENOUGH   ☐ LOVED   ☐ HONEST

Extra Thoughts

Today I'm grateful for:

1
2
3

Date:

How am I today?

Todays weather:

Something Good

Something New

This is how I was kind today:

This is how I was helpful today:

Draw Here

I AM....

☐ BRAVE ☐ KIND

CONFIDENT
☐

☐ HELPFUL ☐ STRONG ☐ SMART

☐ ENOUGH ☐ LOVED ☐ HONEST

Extra Thoughts

Today I'm grateful for:

1

2

3

How am I today?

Todays weather:

Something Good

Something New

This is how I was Kind today:

This is how I was helpful today:

Draw Here

I AM....

☐ BRAVE   ☐ KIND

CONFIDENT
☐

☐ HELPFUL   ☐ STRONG   ☐ SMART

☐ ENOUGH   ☐ LOVED   ☐ HONEST

Extra Thoughts

Today I'm grateful for:

1

2

3

How am I today?

Todays weather:

Something Good

Something New

This is how I was Kind today:

This is how I was helpful today:

Draw Here

I AM....

- ☐ BRAVE
- ☐ KIND
- ☐ CONFIDENT
- ☐ HELPFUL
- ☐ STRONG
- ☐ SMART
- ☐ ENOUGH
- ☐ LOVED
- ☐ HONEST

Extra Thoughts

Today I'm grateful for:

1

2

3

Date:

How am I today?

Todays weather:

Something Good

Something New

This is how I was kind today:

This is how I was helpful today:

I AM....

- ☐ BRAVE
- ☐ KIND
- CONFIDENT ☐
- ☐ HELPFUL
- ☐ STRONG
- ☐ SMART
- ☐ ENOUGH
- ☐ LOVED
- ☐ HONEST

Extra Thoughts

Today I'm grateful for:

1

2

3

How am I today?

Todays weather:

Something Good

Something New

This is how I was kind today:

This is how I was helpful today:

 Draw Here

I AM....

☐ BRAVE ☐ KIND

CONFIDENT ☐

☐ HELPFUL ☐ STRONG ☐ SMART

☐ ENOUGH ☐ LOVED ☐ HONEST

Extra Thoughts

Today I'm grateful for:

1

2

3

How am I today?

Todays weather:

Something Good

Something New

This is how I was kind today:

This is how I was helpful today:

Draw Here

I AM....

☐ BRAVE   ☐ KIND

CONFIDENT
☐

☐ HELPFUL   ☐ STRONG   ☐ SMART

☐ ENOUGH   ☐ LOVED   ☐ HONEST

Extra Thoughts

Today I'm grateful for:

1

2

3

Date:

How am I today?

Todays weather:

Something Good

Something New

This is how I was kind today:

This is how I was helpful today:

 Draw Here

I AM....

☐ BRAVE ☐ KIND

CONFIDENT
☐

☐ HELPFUL ☐ STRONG ☐ SMART

☐ ENOUGH ☐ LOVED ☐ HONEST

Extra Thoughts

Today I'm grateful for:

1

2

3

How am I today?

Todays weather:

Something Good

Something New

This is how I was kind today:

This is how I was helpful today:

Draw Here

I AM....

- ☐ BRAVE
- ☐ KIND
- CONFIDENT ☐
- ☐ HELPFUL
- ☐ STRONG
- ☐ SMART
- ☐ ENOUGH
- ☐ LOVED
- ☐ HONEST

Extra Thoughts

Today I'm grateful for:

1

2

3

Date:

How am I today?

Todays weather:

Something Good

Something New

This is how I was kind today:

This is how I was helpful today:

 Draw Here

I AM....

☐ BRAVE ☐ KIND

CONFIDENT
☐

☐ HELPFUL ☐ STRONG ☐ SMART

☐ ENOUGH ☐ LOVED ☐ HONEST

Extra Thoughts

Today I'm grateful for:

1

2

3

Date:

How am I today?

Todays weather:

Something Good

Something New

This is how I was kind today:

This is how I was helpful today:

Draw Here

I AM....

☐ BRAVE   ☐ KIND

CONFIDENT
☐

☐ HELPFUL   ☐ STRONG   ☐ SMART

☐ ENOUGH   ☐ LOVED   ☐ HONEST

Extra Thoughts

Today I'm grateful for:

1

2

3

How am I today?

Todays weather:

Something Good

Something New

This is how I was Kind today:

This is how I was helpful today:

Draw Here

I AM....

- [ ] BRAVE
- [ ] KIND
- [ ] CONFIDENT
- [ ] HELPFUL
- [ ] STRONG
- [ ] SMART
- [ ] ENOUGH
- [ ] LOVED
- [ ] HONEST

Extra Thoughts

Today I'm grateful for:

1

2

3

How am I today?

Todays weather:

Something Good

Something New

This is how I was kind today:

This is how I was helpful today:

Draw Here

I AM....

☐ BRAVE ☐ KIND

CONFIDENT
☐

☐ HELPFUL ☐ STRONG ☐ SMART

☐ ENOUGH ☐ LOVED ☐ HONEST

Extra Thoughts

Today I'm grateful for:

1

2

3

Date:

How am I today?

Todays weather:

Something Good

Something New

This is how I was kind today:

This is how I was helpful today:

Draw Here

I AM....

- ☐ BRAVE
- ☐ KIND
- ☐ CONFIDENT
- ☐ HELPFUL
- ☐ STRONG
- ☐ SMART
- ☐ ENOUGH
- ☐ LOVED
- ☐ HONEST

Extra Thoughts

Today I'm grateful for:

1

2

3

Date:

How am I today?

Todays weather:

Something Good

Something New

This is how I was kind today:

This is how I was helpful today:

Draw Here

I AM....

☐ BRAVE ☐ KIND

CONFIDENT
☐

☐ HELPFUL ☐ STRONG ☐ SMART

☐ ENOUGH ☐ LOVED ☐ HONEST

Extra Thoughts

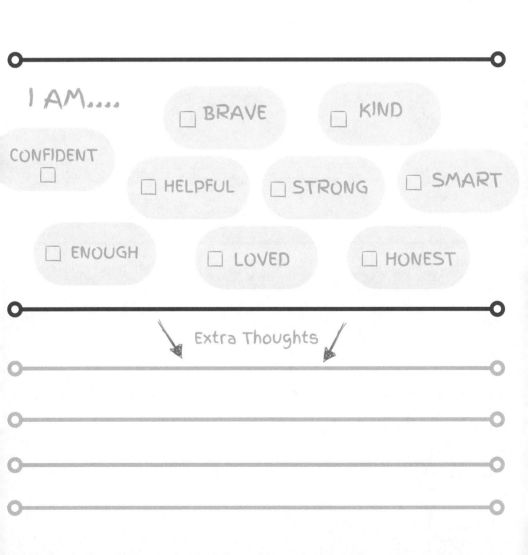

Today I'm grateful for:

1

2

3

Date:

How am I today?

Todays weather:

Something Good

Something New

This is how I was Kind today:

This is how I was helpful today:

Draw Here

I AM....

☐ BRAVE   ☐ KIND

CONFIDENT
☐

☐ HELPFUL   ☐ STRONG   ☐ SMART

☐ ENOUGH   ☐ LOVED   ☐ HONEST

Extra Thoughts

Today I'm grateful for:

1

2

3

How am I today?

Todays weather:

Something Good

Something New

This is how I was kind today:

This is how I was helpful today:

Draw Here

I AM....

☐ BRAVE   ☐ KIND

CONFIDENT
☐

☐ HELPFUL   ☐ STRONG   ☐ SMART

☐ ENOUGH   ☐ LOVED   ☐ HONEST

Extra Thoughts

Today I'm grateful for:

1

2

3

Date:

How am I today?

Todays weather:

Something Good

Something New

This is how I was kind today:

This is how I was helpful today:

Draw Here

I AM....

- [ ] BRAVE
- [ ] KIND
- [ ] CONFIDENT
- [ ] HELPFUL
- [ ] STRONG
- [ ] SMART
- [ ] ENOUGH
- [ ] LOVED
- [ ] HONEST

Extra Thoughts

Today I'm grateful for:

1

2

3

How am I today?

Todays weather:

Something Good

Something New

This is how I was Kind today:

This is how I was helpful today:

Draw Here

I AM....

☐ BRAVE   ☐ KIND

CONFIDENT
☐

☐ HELPFUL   ☐ STRONG   ☐ SMART

☐ ENOUGH   ☐ LOVED   ☐ HONEST

Extra Thoughts

Today I'm grateful for:

1

2

3

How am I today?

Todays weather:

Something Good

Something New

This is how I was Kind today:

This is how I was helpful today:

Draw Here

I AM....

☐ BRAVE   ☐ KIND

CONFIDENT
☐

☐ HELPFUL   ☐ STRONG   ☐ SMART

☐ ENOUGH   ☐ LOVED   ☐ HONEST

Extra Thoughts

Today I'm grateful for:

1

2

3

How am I today?

Todays weather:

Something Good

Something New

This is how I was kind today:

This is how I was helpful today:

Draw Here

I AM....

☐ BRAVE   ☐ KIND

CONFIDENT
☐

☐ HELPFUL   ☐ STRONG   ☐ SMART

☐ ENOUGH   ☐ LOVED   ☐ HONEST

Extra Thoughts

Today I'm grateful for:

1

2

3

Date:

How am I today?

Todays weather:

Something Good

Something New

This is how I was kind today:

This is how I was helpful today:

Draw Here

I AM....

- [ ] BRAVE
- [ ] KIND
- [ ] CONFIDENT
- [ ] HELPFUL
- [ ] STRONG
- [ ] SMART
- [ ] ENOUGH
- [ ] LOVED
- [ ] HONEST

Extra Thoughts

Today I'm grateful for:

1

2

3

How am I today?

Todays weather:

Something Good

Something New

This is how I was kind today:

This is how I was helpful today:

Draw Here

I AM....

☐ BRAVE   ☐ KIND

CONFIDENT
☐

☐ HELPFUL   ☐ STRONG   ☐ SMART

☐ ENOUGH   ☐ LOVED   ☐ HONEST

Extra Thoughts

Today I'm grateful for:

1.

2.

3.

Date:

How am I today?

Todays weather:

Something Good

Something New

This is how I was Kind today:

This is how I was helpful today:

Draw Here

I AM....

☐ BRAVE   ☐ KIND

CONFIDENT
☐

☐ HELPFUL   ☐ STRONG   ☐ SMART

☐ ENOUGH   ☐ LOVED   ☐ HONEST

Extra Thoughts

The End